Byron Sunderland

The Crisis of the Times

A Sermon Preached in the First Presbyterian Church, Washington, D.C.

Byron Sunderland

The Crisis of the Times
A Sermon Preached in the First Presbyterian Church, Washington, D.C.

ISBN/EAN: 9783337087760

Printed in Europe, USA, Canada, Australia, Japan

Cover: Foto ©Lupo / pixelio.de

More available books at **www.hansebooks.com**

THE CRISIS OF THE TIMES:

A SERMON

PREACHED IN THE

First Presbyterian Church,

WASHINGTON, D. C.,

ON THE EVENING OF

THE NATIONAL FAST,

Thursday, April 30, 1863,

BY

Rev. BYRON SUNDERLAND, D. D.

TEXT.—*Isaiah lviii.*, 1–7.—"Cry aloud, spare not, lift up thy voice like a trumpet, and show my people their transgression, and the house of Jacob their sins."

WASHINGTON:
" NATIONAL BANNER" PRESS.
1863.

CORRESPONDENCE.

WASHINGTON, D. C., *May* 2, 1863.

SIR: I have been requested by an association of patriotic citizens to ask of you for publication a copy of your discourse delivered on the evening of the National Fast day, that the thousands who were unable to hear may be permitted to read an authentic copy of that very able and patriotic address.

With great respect,
Your obedient servant,
J. M. EDMUNDS.

REV. BYRON SUNDERLAND.

WASHINGTON, *May* 5, 1863.

Hon. J. M. EDMUNDS:

SIR: Your favor of the 2d instant is just received. The sermon which you request for publication was prepared and delivered under a sense of deep personal responsibility, on the most solemn occasion of our history. So far as it may be read, I devoutly pray its effect to be only and lasting good. With daily supplication for the complete triumph of the Government of the United States, and a glorious future for our beloved though now greatly afflicted country, I remain,

Yours in the bonds of Christian patriotism,
B. SUNDERLAND.

SERMON.

----◆----

ISAIAH lviii., 1-7.—Cry aloud, spare not, lift up thy voice like a trumpet, and show my people their transgression, and the house of Jacob their sins.

Yet they seek me daily and delight to know my ways, as a nation that did righteousness and forsook not the ordinance of their God; they ask of me the ordinances of justice: they take delight in approaching to God.

Wherefore have we fasted, say they, and thou seest not? wherefore have we afflicted our soul, and thou takest no knowledge? Behold, in the day of your fast ye find pleasure, and exact all your labors. Behold, ye fast for strife and debate, and to smite with the fist of wickedness; ye shall not fast as ye do this day, to make your voice to be heard on high.

Is it such a fast that I have chosen, a day for a man to afflict his soul? Is it to bow down his head as a bulrush, and to spread sackcloth and ashes under him? Wilt thou call this a fast and an acceptable day to the Lord?

Is not this the fast that I have chosen? to loose the bands of wickedness, to undo the heavy burdens, and to let the oppressed go free, and that ye break every yoke?

Is it not to deal thy bread to the hungry, and that thou bring the poor that are cast out to thy house? when thou seest the naked that thou cover him; and that thou hide not thyself from thine own flesh?

This day is to me as solemn as a day of judgment. When I think what we, the people of America, our rulers and chief men in all stations, have been professing to do this day, before God and in the sight of all the nations of the earth, I tremble from head to foot, in every joint. What is it that we have been professing to do this day? I have read it to you in the proclamation of the President. How many out of the thirty-two millions of human souls composing this nation have not even pretended to observe the day in form! And of those who have pretended to comply with the request of the proclamation, how many have made of it only a fearful mockery in the sight of God! How few comparatively of all these multitudes has the Omniscient Eye beheld in a suitable and acceptable posture before him! Truly, the heart of man is deceitful above all things and desperately wicked; and who can know it? We may well fear in regard to all of us that it is now as it was before the flood, and that God sees that the wickedness of man is great in the earth, and that every imagination of the thought of his heart is only evil continually. And we may devoutly pray, each one of us all, in the language of the Psalmist, Search me, O God, and know my heart; try me, and know my thoughts, and see if there be any wicked way in me, and lead me in the way everlasting.

If we could think that this day had been kept as a day of holy convocation unto the Lord. in the entire land, or even throughout the borders of the adhering States, and that among all the people it had been observed in the same spirit which was manifest among the Ninevites under the preaching of Jonah, we might at least feel supported by the hope that such a repentance would be followed by immediate and signal displays of divine favor in our behalf. Look for a moment at the record of that event.

"Forty days and Nineveh shall be overthrown!" That was the cry which rung through the city its terrible alarm. That, in substance, is the awful cry which goes out among all nations where human wickedness and corruption have become so fearful as to strike at the very foundations of human society, and to threaten

the demolition of the most stable and the most benefi-
cent structures of human government. This cry is
travelling now through the length and breadth of our
own land, like the travelling prophet in the midst of
Nineveh ; and it has been so travelling for the three days
as of old, and a year for a day. It began afar off in the
fears, the anxieties, the predictions of the wisest and
best men of the nation ; and it waxed nearer and louder,
the awful cry of Heaven's indignation against the land
for its wickedness, until, two years ago it broke in the
thunders of the cannonade at Charleston. Since then,
that cry has been reverberating in the North and in the
South, in the East and in the West—the voice that
thunders at noonday, the voice that startles at mid-
night, the warning of a nation's overthrow, the dissolution of American republican empire. Its echoes are
heard in the sobs and moanings of a hundred thousand
families, over whom a pall of mourning for the slain
has settled. Its accents tremble fearfully in the passions of men, who, animated as by a spirit of diabolical
fury, are ready to inaugurate a storm of anarchy and
violence, compared with which the convulsions of the
physical creation are tame and innocuous. This is our
position to-day ; and that prophet-cry rolls on una-
bated, Wo, wo, wo to the inhabitants of the land! All
the air is full of its portents ; all the signals of providence foreberald its desolations. Nay, the one prophet
voice, that sounded the doom of ancient Nineveh, is now
multiplied into ten thousand times ten thousand voices,
that surge and thunder around and before, above and
behind us, on every side. And the simple meaning of
it now is, as then it was, repentance or ruin. Besotted
and blind with insensibility or infatuation must he be
who cannot now at this late day perceive that this is
our precise condition as individuals and as a nation.

What came next? They believed God—king, nobles, and people. There is a volume of meaning in that short sentence. It opens the secret of all that followed. That is the only remedy for us now; in that is our health. But if this faith in God be confined to a few only, as I fear it is; if, like Abraham pleading for the cities of the plain, and putting one condition after another to narrow the chances of their destruction, they who believe God in this nation at this hour are too few in proportion to the whole to render it by their righteousness worth the saving, then the boldest of us may turn pale, and the most sanguine may despair, for the principles of the Divine government are fixed. God can by no means clear the guilty. He is of one mind, and who can turn Him? When He rises up, who can stand before Him? Oh, that we are now in such a case before Him, and that we have reason to believe that multitudes everywhere in the land have no more personal or practical regard to the voice of His judgments, than to an oldwife's fable, is a fact so appalling as to transcend the power of human expression. Because it augurs that, in spite of all our hopes, and all our faith, and all our desire, we are nevertheless descending every hour and at every step in the path of inevitable and swift destruction. It means simply this, and nothing else. We are at this moment in our national life in a condition like that of a man in his skiff already drawn upon the breakers above Niagara, and already partaking of the speed and drift of that resistless current, which, unless a miracle be interposed, will surely carry him over the precipice. That is our danger, I am persuaded, in our moral and spiritual condition as a nation. But was that the case with Nineveh? Far otherwise; *they believed God.*

And what next? The king, with his nobles, pro-

claimed a fast, and caused it to be published throughout the city, saying, Let every living thing be cast
down, let them not taste drink or food, let them be
clothed in sackcloth and mourn for sin, let them turn
every one from his evil way and from the violence that
is in their hands, and let them cry mightily unto God.
Who can tell if God will turn and repent, and turn
away from His fierce anger, that we perish not? And
after this solemn proclamation of the king, in the sight
of all the people, where do we hear of him next? Not in
scenes of dissolute amusement, not convoking his
chamber of nobles, or reviewing his mighty armies to
make a gala-day of holy time; not recklessly exhibiting
an example in the presence of his subjects which might
least tend to prepare them or him for the solemn period
of mourning to which they had been called. No, this
is not the conduct of the king of Nineveh. He believed
God, and his works corresponded to his faith. He left
nothing to be done by proxy. He saw clearly enough
that his own action would powerfully influence the
action of the population. He was in earnest in the
business of seeking God—in calling the city over which
he ruled, to avert the threatened calamity, by the one
way of appointment, which has ever been open to all
the generations of men. And so we are told that he
arose from his throne and laid his robe from him, and
covered him with sackcloth and sat in ashes That
was his position before God and in the sight of the
nation in that day of humiliation.

And what next? All the people followed his example. There is probably nothing on record equal to
this repentance of Nineveh for its thoroughness and
universality. It was genuine, radical, efficacious.
There was no concealment, no hypocrisy, no mockery
then. It was heart-felt, rational, and entire. It moved

all minds; struck at the plague of every man's heart: reformed every soul of all the multitudes of the city. It was a moral miracle of the grace and power of God, imbuing a whole population suddenly with a sense of sin—with a sense of duty and obligation to God—and the most profound conviction of dependence upon Him and of hope only in His mercy. It was that repentance which transformed them—made them a different community from what they were before—made them new creatures—changed all their habits of feeling, thought, and conduct—changed their principles, their views, their motives, their life—brought them to renounce their former profligacy and return to the path of purity, soberness, and peace. They believed and embraced the truth of God just so far, just so fast as it was made known to them. They entered directly upon the obedience of this faith. They espoused the cause of the right, and set their faces as a flint against everything false and wrong. They became a righteous people, by the putting away, every one of them, their iniquities.

Now, in this respect, it was not with them as, I fear, it is with us. Their repentance was individual and personal, as well as federative and national. But we; how do we feel? Has every human being in this nation to-day, capable of reflection and capable of knowing and understanding his relation and duties to God, solemnly considered and reviewed the delinquencies and transgressions of his past life, and devoutly purposed, God helping him, to be a better man in the future; to lead a life of Christian piety and prayer, and to let all men know that henceforth he no longer halts between two opinions—henceforth he is on the Lord's side, in life, in death, and to all eternity? The man who has not come up to that mark and standard this day, I pronounce, in so far, an enemy of God and his country. The man who has failed to do that, has signally failed to answer the end for which this day was appointed; and for the mode in which it has been met by us God will hold each one to a solemn and fearful accountability. We cannot appoint these days of national humiliation and prayer in the sight of mankind, as we have done one after the other in time past, and trifle with their very meaning and intention, with impunity. If we undertake to do this, we shall find out to our sorrow that we are wrestling with One who can easily overthrow us, One who will see, that in our obduracy and blindness, we are utterly ground to powder. The Ninevites seem to have thoroughly comprehended. the significance of this, and they kept the fast, not merely in the outward forms of humiliation, but in the spirit and the soul, in verity and truth. They realized and illustrated, in their experience and by their example, the very nature of that fast which is here so emphatically commended in our text, and which is alone the fast that is acceptable to God.

And then what next? God saw their works that they turned from their evil way, and God repented of the evil that he had said that he would do unto them, and he did it not. Oh! the unutterable tenderness and fidelity of the Divine placability. Go see the old father hanging with tears of compassion and joy upon the neck of his long-lost son. That is God in all the constraining mercies of his unutterable love. That is the great and terrible One in the heavens, in whose anger is infinite might, in whose wrath is desolating and withering power. But what He is to the contumacious, that He is not to the believing, the penitent, and sincere. To those who by patient continuance in well-doing, are chosen to stand before Him, everything in the being, the character, the attributes, the law, the government, the purposes and providence of God, is friendly. For them and for their final triumph, He has stored the universe. They shall never be confounded. All things shall work for their good. But to the evil, all shall work for evil. The very slumber of God's wrath, His yearning His weeping, all shall turn at last into the fierceness of indignation against them. What then is the alternative? Where do we stand? The point to be remembered is, not whether the Lord is on our side, but whether we are on the Lord's side. The simple question before us this day is not whether God will withdraw his judgments, but whether we are an incorrigible people. That is the whole sum and substance of it, and that is the issue now to be tried; it is the very thing which constitutes the gist and stress of our present condition and experience. If, as time rolls on and the alarm of ruin is sounded in our ears, we will neither heed nor hear it; if we will shut our eyes persistently and madly to all the proofs and tokens of the Divine displeasure; if we will not learn nor comprehend the lessons of our duty and obligation; if we will refuse to inquire of God what he would have us to do; and if when truth is shown us we will not embrace it, will not espouse it, will not stand by it, will not defend it at all hazards and costs, albeit even to the giving up of life; if we are and continue to be so indifferent to God's cause in the earth, so inconsiderate, so hard of heart, so blind and perverse, so brutish and benighted as not to see nor perceive nor know the things which belong to our true peace, why then, of course, we must be destroyed; there is no other alternative; we may as well make up our minds to it at once. He that spared not his own Son will not spare the guilty nations of the earth. He, that in tears of bitter anguish stood by and saw Jerusalem utterly wasted, will also stand by and see this country ruined, if we as a people shall continue incorrigible.

While stating in this broad form my conviction of this fearful doctrine, I am aware there is another principle on which God sometimes proceeds in His administration over the affairs of men, and in His disposition of the communities and nations of the earth, and that is—He does sometimes interpose to save a multitude from impending destruction, or to postpone a public calamity for the sake of a few, or even sometimes of one of His faithful servants. Thus when Moses plead for the life of his nation, God turned from the purposed destruction for the time; and so when Solomon in his old age had defiled the land with idolatry, God threatened the rending of the kingdom, but postponed it to the succeeding reign for the sake of David his father. But this is the fearful law of all human iniquity, that sooner or later its retribution must come. Vengeance upon sin, though long delayed and slumbering long, must come at last, in spite of all the memories of the pious dead or of all the tears and prayers of the pious living. There must come a day in the history of every incorrigible people when God says my spirit shall no longer strive with man. Ephraim is joined to his idols; let him alone. Though Moses and Samuel stood before me, yet my mind could not be toward this people. And when that day comes, it is the old story of Egypt and Babylon, of Assyria and Greece and Rome, under the philosophy and religion of Paganism; and it is the more modern story of the European and American nations under the dispensation of Christianity. It is a day of pride and luxury and fulness of bread, a day of the laxity of all moral discipline and the perversion of all moral principle, a day of individual and social debauchery and corruption, a day when the very thoughts of men are twisted and turned out of the way, and human nature, salacious, infidel and irreligious, even amid all the circumstances of outward refinement and intellectual development, presents a spectacle of apostacy at once the most disgusting and the most alarming. When society reaches this point, as I verily believe it has this day in our country, there is but one of two things that must speedily follow: either a repentance and reformation approaching that of Nineveh, or ruin and destruction, remediless and condign.

All this is clearly set forth in this message of Isaiah. God deals with us as with rational beings. He is full of succor and salvation towards us if we are only resolved on simply doing right. In this posture of mind everything is favorable. God has so constituted his universe that we have no cause for fear or alarm, no cause to bow down our head as a bulrush or cover ourselves with sackcloth, or to spend a day in the abasing and servile affliction of the soul, or in making our faces long and sad, when we have once closed the struggle with ourselves, and have come to the firm determination to do exactly right. It is only before this self-struggle is concluded, and while we are yet in the bondage and pollution of sin and guilt and condemnation, that we may justly fear. While we seek to conceal our sin, to cover up our iniquity, to cancel it by atonements and penances and prayers, instead of freely and fully confessing and forsaking it, then it is that we may observe all the outward formalities of religion, and still wonder why God does not regard us, nor hear our prayer. Nothing but honesty before God, nothing but truth and sincerity will do in a case like ours. We may perform the cere-

monies of confession and supplication, we may go
without food for a day, we may cover ourselves with
sackcloth, and vainly endeavor to appease our own
conscience or attract upon ourselves the favorable
notice of the Searcher of all hearts, but He knows all
the time that our approaches to Him are only in appearance and in word, while our hearts are far from
Him. He knows that what we do in the performance
of the services of religion, we do for a cover of our
wickedness, and for a salvo to a wounded conscience,
but not as the expression of a broken heart and a con-
trite spirit. We fast, indeed, we afflict ourselves for
a day, but we repent of nothing in all this; we fast
for debate and strife, and to smite with the fist of wickedness, and yet we wonder that God takes no knowledge of all our pains. How can He recognize such a
state of mind, and such a spirit, as the fast which He
has chosen? There is no truth in it, no reformation
in it, no forsaking of sin, no real confession of wrong
whatever. Therefore, God cannot recognize such a
fast. He must loathe and abhor it, and turn it into
a more bitter curse.

But the prophet vividly draws the contrast between
a true fast and this mockery. "Is not this the fast that
I have chosen—to loose the bands of wickedness, to undo
the heavy burdens, and to let the oppressed go free,
and that ye break every yoke? Is it not to deal thy
bread to the hungry, and to bring the poor that are
cast out to thy house, to take away the yoke, the putting forth of the finger, and speaking vanity? Is it
not to turn away thy foot from the Sabbath, from doing
thy pleasure on my holy day; and to call the Sabbath
a delight, the holy of the Lord, honorable: and shall
honor him, not doing thine own ways, nor finding thine
own pleasure?" What a contrast there is in a fast like

this! Here is the devout and filial recognition and reverence of God and of His law and ordinances. Here is the separation of the soul and of society from the vices and iniquities that have defiled and corrupted them. Here is the positive abandonment of selfishness and covetousness, of violence, cruelty, and oppression in all their forms. Here is the ceasing from vices and evils which contaminate and degrade, and from all sentiments, opinions, prejudices, habits, practices, and customs of a pernicious tendency, and of a doubtful propriety in all relations and among all classes of human beings. And here are the opposite dispositions, virtues, and charities which constitute the cap-sheaf and the crown of all our usefulness, and all our happiness both here and hereafter. God presents this contrast of moral and spiritual attributes of human character as the very soul and substance of all acceptable sacrifice, prayer, and worship; and upon the presence or absence of these elements in a day like this, depends the issue of its observance.

There is at this point another momentuos truth which adds solemnity to our present national posture in the sight of heaven and before the eyes of all men. It is that no nation that ever existed has sinned against such light as this nation. The degree of light against which a people go on to sin is a most important element in determining the grade or extent of guilt or heinousness which must be estimated as belonging to its offences. Tried by this rule, no people were ever so guilty as we have been. When Nineveh repented, she had only before her eyes the example of the cities of the plain and some of the earlier catastrophes of human sin. When Jerusalem was destroyed, it was even then before the day of the Christian Era had fairly begun to shine. But we, we who live in the light of the nineteenth century, and

upou whom History has poured all its examples, and
Providence all its illustrations, and Inspiration all its
instructions; we who have lived in the shining faces
of all God's angels of truth and ministers of grace;
we who have basked in the summer sun-light of
an unclouded Gospel; we who have looked morning,
noon, and night upon the glorious walking of the
Sun of Righteousness; we who have been taught
from infancy the simple but sublime principles of the
Christian faith—of God and eternity, human life, duty,
and destiny—we have sinned against the light of the
Sermon on the Mount, against the light of all the
evangelists and epistles of the New Testament, against
the light of the Reformation and our own Revolution,
against the grandest and most glorious age of Christian charities and missions the world has ever seen,
against the light of eighty years of unparalleled pros-
perity, against the light of all its science, its learning,
its discovery, its discussion, its mighty franchise.
We have sinned, while holding in trust the noblest
heritage ever held by any people, while having charge
in effect of the last and most precious hopes of human
nature. And now through our follies and sins we have
brought ourselves to the verge of ruin, and unless God
in his infinite mercy shall swiftly interpose through
mysteries of His providence and grace higher and
deeper than any we have ever known, to prevent the
calamity, we shall plunge over and sink, one and all,
into an abyss of shame and infamy such as no people
ever contracted, not even the doomed and wandering
house of Israel.

   This, as I humbly conceive it, is our condition to-
day. We are to be tried upon the principle of the
degree of light we have enjoyed; and so tried we cannot but see that wherein the nation has sinned, it is

in these regards the foremost sinner among all the nations of history.

And now it is said in the word of God that when His judgments are abroad in the earth, the inhabitants of the world will learn righteousness. Let us consider whether those judgments are abroad among us, for our sins—and if so, what they are, and how many, and how heavy; for God suits His judgments to our sins—makes our sins, indeed, the punishment of themselves. This is that which gives to retribution its fearful power. We are, as a people, under a heavy hand. The principal feature of these judgments is that we have been left to ourselves; we have been left to be filled with the fruit of our own doings. They are not the judgments of famine or pestilence or earthquakes, the invisible and wasting scourges which go over the earth decimating and destroying, by a law too subtle for our tracing and too secret for our penetration. But they proceed from the shock and collision of human agencies, directed and impelled by the conflicting sentiments and passions which lie behind them. They stand before us in all the woes and horrors of a bitter, protracted, desolating civil war. From the forum of peaceful discussion and republican suffrage, the controversy has been carried to the last resort of physical force, violence, and blood. And this has been done under circumstances and with concomitants of evil such as to affect the whole mind and heart of the nation with every form of affliction and mental distress. Upon the more open and tangible effects of such a civil war as this, in its bearing upon the disruption of business, the destruction of property and even the loss of human life, it is not my purpose to dwell. The shock thus given to the country, the disorder it produces, the derangement and uncertainty

it occasions, the burdens it imposes, and the fortunes
it destroys, are all matters with which the people of
this country are but too sadly familiar. And yet even
in these things, through all the regions of the adhering, with the exception of the border States, these
judgments of God have thus far been tempered with
singular mercy, and have on the general scale been
marvellously mitigated. Indeed, so far in the controversy, it is to be feared that the people inhabiting
these sections of the Republic, thro' their comparative
exemption from the storm, do not even yet take to
heart the awful nature of the judgments now smiting
the land, nor comprehend the extent and depth of
their complicity in the sins which have culminated in
this fury. I make all allowance, indeed, for what
they have done and borne and sacrificed; but when it
is all subtracted, the present thrift, and drift, and
appearance, and action, and condition of the people
in all those regions, constitute a ground of wonder
and amazement at the long suffering and tender mercy
of our God. It is, indeed, upon the people of the
border States, and throughout the region where the
sway of the rebellion is still rigid and unbroken, that
the woes and miseries of this tempest have hitherto
been falling heaviest. And when we do but try to
conceive the depths of the sorrow of the true and faithful people in these regions, and to contemplate even
one tithe of what they have suffered in their most keen
and sacred sensibilities, no power of words can express
fully the nature and extent of their wretchedness.
The disruption of business associations, the separation
of families, the social ostracism, the fearful aliena-
tions of human hearts, the cruelties perpetrated, the
scenes of persecution, the grinding heel of despotism,
the awful profanity and jocularity of death in his

murderous round, surely nothing in the horrors of the French Revolution can be said to have transcended the miseries and anguish of men, women, and children whose only provocation to the tormentors is their unchanging love and devotion for the Union and Government of their fathers. The same spirit, though in a form as yet modified and restrained, we have witnessed and felt here in the very Capital of the country.. The lines of division have run right through old and long established friendships, have sundered pastors and people, have made a man's foes even them of his own household, and have engendered the bitterness and fostered the prejudices that ever walk forth as the premonitory spectres of social and ecclesiatical dissolution. So that the question is no longer a mere question of party politics, or preference for a candidate, or a question of some measure of sectional or local policy, but it is a question of fundamental character, a question of human right and duty, a question of human conscience, a question of the life and death of a mighty nation; and along with this there are questions of the most amazing and appalling complication and difficulty, all arising from the confusion and variety of public sentiment, and from the moral obliquity and perversion of the national mind and heart. The very things which now strain and try this nation are traceable to the sins of the nation. It is not ignorance that is trying us now, but wilful, wanton blindness, unreasoning selfishness, and the practical atheism of the people, from which as from an exhaustless fountain rolls the current of our follies, our errors, and our crimes—passion and prejudice, suspicion, jealousy, lust for power, avarice, intrigue, hatred, rancor, all inflamed and aggravated by the open venality and flagrant wickedness of the public press.

Political confusion and judicial blindness are the real judgments which now lie upon the land, which now confuse and bewilder those who would be honest, who desire to be true, who want nothing in this controversy but what is right, but what is in accordance with the will and law of God, and who would gladly do what they may to establish the institutions of the Government upon a sure foundation of public righteousness; who feel that it is no time for sophistries and technicalities, for quibbles and formalities, but who go for the substance of doctrine, the eternal righteousness of God in all the relations of man to his fellow-man, as well as of men to God. And because we are confounded in these things, and do not even yet know whether a lie is in our right hand, we are still groping and stumbling on the dark mountains of sin and shame, our eyes blinded, our ears heavy, our hearts hardened, and our hands paralyzed; we are as a nation in a swound, feeling the sharp sting of God's goads spurring us out of our stupor, but yet drowsy and but a little awake, only seeing men as trees walking, and filled with the pains and agonies, not, we hope, of a second death, but of a second birth. This it seems to me is our condition under the present judgments of Heaven.

And now we have no right to shut our eyes to the sins which form the ground of indictment against us. We are guilty if we attempt to do this, guilty in the attempted concealment; and we are really the more culpable if, on an occasion like this, we undertake to blink or flinch from the full acknowledgment and recognition of any one of the sins of which we as individuals, or as communities, or as a nation have been guilty in the sight of heaven. But where shall we begin the catalogue of these iniquities? It is even difficult to classify and document them. With a language copious in terms significant of human iniquities, we should exhaust the vocabulary of our mother-tongue long before we could express the full tale of our private and public delinquencies—sins of the heart, sins of the spirit, sins of the flesh, sins of ignorance and sins of wantonness, sins of omission and sins of commission, secret sins and open sins, personal sins and social sins, sins in the family and sins in the church, sins in business life, sins in fashionable life, sins in private life and sins in official life, sins political and sins ecclesiastical. In all these forms of human depravity, the terrific principle of spiritual wickedness seeks its manifestation.

All sin is fiery, and eats as doth a canker. It riddles out the very basis of moral character in man; it frets and wears away the warp and woof of the confidences and securities of human life; it is the moral *azote*. Nothing of spiritual purity can live in its presence; under its impulse and dominion men have their lusts excited, their passions inflamed, their understandings darkened, their consciences seared, and their hearts hardened. So prepared they enter upon life, and in the choice of avocations, of associates, of aims, and of means to those aims, they are constantly exposed to powerful temptations which break down all moral restraint, and send them on in a career of immorality, impiety, and dishonesty, which not only proves their own ruin, but seriously tends to injure and corrupt all with whom they come in contact. Out of all this mass of human iniquity certain cardinal forms of human sin and profligacy appear.

In defining national offences, each man must pursue his own method, and make his own distinctions. I am not disposed to be over nice, or careful, in adher-

ing strictly to technical or theological terms, or the pop-
ular phraseology of the day. I shall consider those sins
national which are known as open, public, or general, whether in a form organized or unorganized. I
shall consider those as national sins which involve the
great majority of the people in their practice, their
motive, or their sympathy. On the subject of private
and personal sins, which are to be confessed and re-
paired in a manner corresponding to their nature, I
need not now undertake, as it would be manifestly
impossible, to dwell, any further than to say that the
whole aggregate of them, no doubt, furnishes one
serious and solemn reason for the private and public
afflictions that are resting on all the land. But there
are some general and positive forms of sin which it
would, in my judgment, be the sheerest hypocrisy to
overlook on a day like this.

I. And the first I mention is the practical rejection
of the Gospel of Jesus Christ by vast numbers of the
people. This is so general that it amounts, in my
estimation, to a national sin of the deepest dye.
It is tantamount to a charge of irreligion, impiety
and atheism, and is the sin for which every man who
stands in it is now arraigned before God. This is
their condemnation, that light has come into the world
and men have chosen darkness rather than light, because their deeds are evil. He that believeth not on
Christ is condemned already. For the testimony of
Christ is the spirit of prophecy; and that is no less
than the infinite spirit of truth, the spirit of God, the
Holy Ghost. We have quenched that spirit and ex-
tinguished its light. We have mocked at it until we
are become vain and empty. We are no longer able
to conquer, because God and His Christ have become a
myth to us, and we have cast away the only might that

makes men and nations strong. I believe in my soul that God is angry with this nation, and is now bringing us into judgment because we have so many of us failed to confess Jesus Christ before men, and to receive His spiritual kingdom into our hearts with all its laws, agencies, influences, and effects. And I put this first and foremost, because it is a practical denial of God in the kingdom of His grace, and in the last means and methods He ever designs to employ for the recovery and salvation of mankind. It is, in effect, utterly ignoring his prerogative, despising his authority, and setting at nought his very mercy and compassion. It is the deepest insult, and the foulest dishonor, we can ever pay to him, because under the present dispensation it prepares the way for every other iniquity in the catalogue of human guilt.

II. Again, I mention idolatry as a cardinal sin of which we have, in many forms, been guilty. It follows that if men, who must have some object of sovereign desire to which they pay supreme devotion, will not have God for that object, they will, virtually, dethrone Him in their hearts, and establish there some idol-god of the current age. We have all had gods of one kind or other before the Lord God Jehovah, and we have worshipped our idol, whatever it be, without regard to the claims, the commandment, or the statutes of the one only true and everliving God. I believe that He is angry with us for this, and that His indignation is now smoking against us, and against all our idol deities that we have cherished in the land.

III. Again, I mention the general neglect and violation of God's ordinances, the sabbath, and the sanctuary, and the profanation of His name. The whole air is loaded with a foul-mouthed profanity: and in fact all this is accompanied by a degree of levity, vulgarity, and vanity, that are as appalling as they are well nigh universal. Men who profess to be loyal to their country, openly and shamelessly trample on the sabbath, and provoke Him to anger who has said, I will not hold him guiltless that taketh my name in vain. I believe God is angry with us for this, and that His anger smokes, and will smoke, upon the profane and impious race of men who treat the whole subject of Christianity, with its requirements and restraints, as a mere story, an idle song, who conduct in regard to it as if it were only a figment or fiction of the past.

IV. Again, I mention the general corruption of manners and morals which is manifest in vice and dissipation, in excess, extravagance, and intemperance, everywhere—in the highest circles of fashion, in the lowest dens of infamy—and all this fostered and catered to by the bold and reckless corruptors of society, while the well nigh total failure to correct, restrain, or extinguish the public profligacy of the times, either by family and primary instruction, by a Christian public sentiment, by the laws of the land, or through the officers of the Government itself, is a delinquency so great as to enhance our criminality, and increase the evils of our condition a thousand fold. There is no doubt but we are suffering from these evils in all the ramifications of human society ; and in this respect, if God's wrath be not turned away by timely repentance, we must share the fate of every other people whose very luxuries and licenses have first enervated, and finally destroyed them.

V. I mention again the spirit of cruelty and oppression which has marked the white race of America

2

toward the Indian and the African. When the chapter
of our usurpations and perfidies toward the aborigines
of this country shall be fully disclosed, we shall find,
I greatly fear, that notwithstanding the treacherous
and savage dispositions, and occasional outbreaks of
the barbarians, the refinements of infamy which the
dominant race have practiced upon them are not less
repugnant to truth and justice, or heinous in the sight
of God. And then as to the evils and wrongs of human
bondage—when I come to speak upon this subject I am
well aware that I touch the sensitive nerve, the sore
spot, of this whole nation. And yet though I should
encounter the settled convictions or prejudices of every
man in the nation, I feel that I should not have per-
formed my whole duty this day without plainly setting
before you my estimate of the subject as it appears to
me in the present light; and when I have done this as
briefly as possible, I shall feel that I have finished my
testimony in respect to this question by exhausting, so
far as I am able, the obligation that rests upon me.

First, then, I believe that the system of slavery as
it has existed in our country when considered only in
the light of the consequences that have followed it,
has been an evil and a curse of the most appalling
magnitude and enormity. To say nothing of its inci-
dental or inherent and essential wrongs upon the
African race, and after abating its alleged, fancied,
or real advantages as an institution of human society,
it is, as I firmly believe, nothing short of the solemn
truth of God to declare that it has been "the apple
of discord," among the ruling race, that has wrought
more dissension, more animosity, and more lasting
bitterness and woe, than any one, or all other causes
combined since the foundation of the Government.
The traces of this evil are in the Federal Consti-

tution, legislation, and history of the country: but the spirit of the evil lies back of all written or documentary instruments; lies in the unsanctified mind, and heart, and passions of man; lies in commercial cupidity, and ambition for political aristocracy and power. And, therefore, I do not believe that any one portion of the people in any one section of the land are alone to be blamed, or held accountable, for whatever of sin or suffering this system may have entailed upon us. ˙ Since the war broke out, and the great events of its progress thus far have transpired. I am disposed to stand equally amazed at the proofs of human insincerity on the one hand, and the claims of divine authority on the other. I am constrained to censure the injustice of the laws of exclusion against this outcast portion of God's human creatures, and to denounce the cruel, preposterous, and inexorable prejudice in which these laws are founded. I believe, in short, that the all-seeing eye of God beholds a degree of selfishness, hypocrisy, inconsistency, and false philanthropy upon this subject which positively amounts to the infatuation and frenzy of judicial blindness among all the people East and West, North and South, and which of itself would be sufficient to sink the whole nation into the nethermost pit of perdition. And after long years of angry and embittered controversy, in which men have not known the manner of spirit they were of, this great, fearful, complicated mass of guilt and misery, this awful nightmare and incubus which was lying across the very vitals of the nation which no skill or foresight of human wisdom could remedy or relieve, has been thrown into the mighty scales of civil war, and the sword of God is unsheathed to cut the knot of this more than Gordian mystery; and to rip from the heart of the nation

the disguises that have hidden our own real condition from our eyes; and to solve in unanticipated ways,
and by means we never could have foreseen, the questions connected with this subject which have hitherto
been both our torment and our shame. I believe that
the time had come when nothing but war was left to
open our eyes to our true moral state in the sight of
God, and to educate the mind and heart of the nation
to a new platform of doctrine, sentiment, and opinion, on this as well as on every other great interest of
mankind in the advancing day of a Christian civilization. I believe it is the design of God that the system of African slavery shall pass away, and that the
true era of its decline was struck when the first gun
of the rebellion made its booming salutation to the
brave Anderson and his little band under the case-
mates of Sumter. And because I have been impressed
with this belief from the beginning, and as occasion
offered expressed it, there are those in this community who branded me with what I imagine they sup-
pose to be the vilest and most odious of epithets, and
who regarded me as having wholly departed from the
walks of clerical propriety. Here, then, I define my
position. I am in favor of abolishing all human sin
and wrong-doing, whether it be in connection with
the black laws of the free States, or the slave laws of
the South—whether it be in connection with Sabbath
breaking, profanity, or whatever else may tend to mar
and degrade human nature, and to provoke against us
the just judgments of Heaven. I am in favor of such
abolition, in short, as is announced in this passage
from the prophet, and sanctioned by the favor of the
Lord God Almighty, and let the man who dissents
from this position stand up on this great day and pro-
duce his reasons. If it is this to be an abolitionist,

then I am an abolitionist. And I can afford here to
wait and suffer all the present consequences of such
a declaration, in the firm conviction that the day is
not far distant when it will be no longer regarded as
a crime, or even as an indiscretion, for a man to stand
up here, or in any other portion of the country, and
plead truly and faithfully for God and his fellow
men.

VI. And now once more I mention another crying
and crushing sin that we have to deplore and lament
to-day—the sin of secession and rebellion against the
Government of the United States, and the connivance
of secret sympathizers and abettors. I regard this as
a high crime against God and man; not a mere mis-
take or misfortune, save where men and women are
compelled or constrained to act in the character of
traitors and rebels by the despotic mandate of the
arch-conspirators against the integrity, the peace,
and safety of the Federal Union. That there was a
foul and shameful conspiracy, attended by the inso-
lence and ferocity of fiends in human shape, first to
assassinate the President-elect on his way to the Capital, and afterwards to seize the city and murder
Union men, women, and children, there is not the
slightest doubt; and if the secret history of the plots
of these men could come to light, it would no doubt.
startle the whole nation with the horrors of these con-
templated atrocities. And if we look at the persecution and distress inflicted on the innocent wherever
the ruthless perjurers have been able to hold their
sway, we shall find that not in all the annals of mar-
tyrdom have our heroic and faithful countrymen been
transcended by examples either in the lofty spirit of
their devotion or in the brutal and bloody savagery
2*

of their oppressors. And yet this Government has been unable or unwilling to afford them any relief, while it shields, and protects, and feeds with almost criminal indulgence the secret enemies of its existence who live beneath the shadows of its very Capitol, detesting it in its magnanimity, and applauding the open Treason which with an armed front is clutching at its very throat. Amazed at such a state of things, I sometimes wonder what posterity will think in the clear light of a coming day which I pray may succeed the darkness of the present night, in contemplation of the subtlety and the depth of the treachery that pervades every nook and corner, and whether they will be more astonished at the madness of disloyalty in its perversion of the plainest principle of common honesty and duty, or at the toleration and clemency of a government which through years of suffering, disaster, and humiliation, still fails not to cherish in its bosom this nest of vipers. Nor am I constrained to speak thus of a portion of our community from any spirit or desire of personal violence or capital retribution but such as the necessities of the general safety and of self-preservation imperatively demand. I only feel that the community ought to be cleared of the spirit of disloyalty, by a division of those whose hearts are with the South in this rebellion from those whose hearts are with the Government up to the full standard of scriptural obedience. This is the only way that I recognize in which we can repent of and forsake the sin of sedition and revolt.

Those who feel at heart no allegiance to the Government should be put beyond the lines at least. That is the gentlest visitation that the authorities can lawfully bestow; for this is no question of party politics, and I deny the impeachment of it in the most emphatic terms. It is purely a question of religious duty which we owe to God and our country. And if we mean to forsake our sins, if we mean to put away from among us the abominable thing, if we mean to return unto God with all our hearts, we must recur to the law of the Bible: if thine eye offend thee pluck it out; if thine hand offend thee cut it off. Nay, nay, we have before us, in this passage from the prophet, the true solution of the issues that are pending.

And this is called preaching politics. Now, when the ship of state, freighted as it is with all our memories and all our hopes, lies tossing in the tempest; when it is no longer a question of policy or preference as between rival parties and candidates in time of peace, but a deeper, broader, more vital question of the triumph of the Government and the *conscience* of the American people over a system of usurpation and despotism, sustained by an organized and armed rebellion against them—now, when a fierce and bloody attempt is made to undermine the very foundations of social order and to pull down the noblest structure of empire the sun has ever shone upon, and to sunder a land that was once most happy in all the arts and industries of advancing civilization, and to blot out from the face of the globe the unity of a mighty nation and to impair forever the greatness and the usefulness of a people among whom the divine principles and precepts of Christianity itself have had their freest and their noblest scope—would it not be thought a thing incredible that the Christian people and the Christian ministry of this land should stand aloof, should manifest a deep and profound indifference, should undertake to live and act and preach and speak and think and feel as though there were no war, and no judgment of God among us whatever? And all this, too, while the whole history of the nation hitherto has been marked by one continued succession of providential interpositions for deliverance, one constant series of examples of the presence and influence of the Christian element in working out our national destiny. Without Christianity, the story of America never could have been told; these manifold and mighty monuments which cover the land could never have been reared. None but God can tell the effect of Christian prayer and fidelity, in the testimony of Christian truth, upon the fortunes of this nation. And now, in such a land, with such a record and such a prospect, and in such a condition, when we feel and know that blows are being struck which, if not repelled, must not only destroy our civil heritage, but also roll back the chariot of human salvation for a thousand years, can the disciples and ministers of this Religion, which has more than all other things made the land a blessing, be excused from the duties and trials which now rest upon the nation? Nay, do you not look to the Christian sentiment and opinion of this country for countenance and support? Do you not rely on the loyalty and the prayers of the Christian people of this country as constituting under God the firmest and most unwavering prop and pillar of the nation's strength? If this be so, then I am here to declare, in the name of the Christian church, and of all that follow the great Head of the church in this land, that as they have never, heretofore, been found wanting in the hour of the country's need, so they will not now be found wanting. For, when it comes to this, the old Religion, which has, for eighteen hundred years, produced the heroes and martyrs of the world, will rise again and lead her mighty processions into the thickest of the contest. And not till the church of Christ has been utterly overthrown, and not until her last prayer goes out, and her last soul is offered upon the altar of expiring liberty, will it be time for men to say "there is no longer any hope." And not until then, can the cause of America, which we believe to be the cause of human nature everywhere, be ruined. And for this reason it is, that in the name of the church we lift up our voice—cry aloud and spare not—showing the people their sins and transgressions. The Christian mind of this nation beholds the spectacle we now present with a feeling of the deepest solemnity and the most painful suspense. The Christian mind of this nation interprets the afflictions we are suffering now, as the judgments of God for our moral obliquity. It holds, that there is righteousness which exalteth a nation, while sin is a reproach to any people. It holds that, in a crisis like this, there is but one inspiration that can carry us through in triumph, and that is the inspiration of the Almighty. It holds that, among the first signs of the presence of such an inspiration is the general return of the people to sobriety and virtue; and therefore it views with pain and grief, with apprehension and alarm, the almost universal reign of vice, vulgarity, and impurity. And because the nation has been so long blind and indifferent to the principles of truth, and so long disobedient to the authority of God, He has not only kindled the fire of this furnace, but he is adding fuel to the flames, and holding us in them, that we may be either purified or consumed. That is the issue now before us—purification or destruction. It is comparatively of little account what may be the tidings from the great sieges or the battle-fields of our military or naval operations: what may be the condition of the currency; or the result of local elections; or, indeed, what may be the daily contingencies or details that fall out to us in the history of this great time; but the true question is, whether, amid all these millions of human beings, a sufficient number may be found upon whom the inspiration of the Almighty has descended, to render it consistent with his most gracious purpose and with the character of his supreme government over men, to interpose and give us the victory, If this point, in the moral and religious condition of the American people can be attained, then we have no fear for the remainder. The same power that delivered the Hebrew nation with a high hand and a stretched out arm; the same power that shielded the people of the Netherlands against the combined attack of the greatest Potentates of the time in Europe; the same power that brought our fathers through the bloody baptism of the Revolution, and gave to them, to bequeath to us, their children, this glorious inheritance, will thunder for us along all our lines of battle, and put our enemies to rout and confusion forever.

I have this faith, then, in the overruling providence of God, and, so believing, let me implore my fellow-countrymen to pause this day and consider how we may best serve our country and our Christ in this time of their need; for a bitter curse fell upon Meroz because they came not up—not up to the help of the Lord against the mighty; and I honestly believe that a deep and bitter curse will fall upon that man, that family, that community, that church, or that city that will now draw back from following the Lord in the pathway of his present providence over this nation. How, then, can you save America in this hour of *wrath*—men, women and children, young men, old men, all men? He is the truest patriot and best lover of his country, the wisest and most efficient friend and helper, who is the most consistent, earnest, and prayerful Christian. If you would serve the cause of your country, cease to do evil and learn to do well; let the wicked forsake his way and the unrighteous man his thoughts; if you have received a bribe, restore it; if you have profaned the name of God, abandon it; if you have trampled on the Sabbath day, trample on it no more; if one have been an infidel, a debauchee, or an inebriate, if one have acted dishonestly, suppressed the truth, corrupted others, defrauded men of their rights, do it no more. Oh! become once again a true man, abandon every vice and every iniquity; be a *man*, sobered and chastened by the great realities and severities of the time—a man no longer for the levity and vain dalliance of the past, but full of the mighty thoughts and stern resolves and steady purposes of present duty. We cannot any longer trifle before God. These are days of sacrifice—the days of heroic suffering—the days of many and most noble martyrdoms. Oh! look at the spectacle of the altars and the holocausts which are now smoking to heaven in all the land, in the very centre of which are lifted up in our American Switzerland the mountains of Tennessee where crackle the hottest fires of the great persecution. The day of peace is gone from us; God only knows when, or if ever, it may return to this generation. Let us compose and prepare ourselves for the sacrifice; let us look defeat, disaster, and even death, if need be, steadily and calmly in the face; but grasping the pillars of God's eternal truth and justice, and holding up our country and all its interests before His throne, let us entreat Him to turn us from our transgressions, that iniquity may not be our ruin. The host of God, bearing the ark of our sacred institutions, and waving the standard of a mighty people in this last exodus of civil and religious liberty, is now already on its march. The trumpets of Providence have summoned the millions of our country to its peril and its toil. The pillar of fire by night and of cloud by day is moving before us. We are standing face to face with God. While His majesty fills us with awe, may His mercy arm us with strength to live and labor, to watch and pray, to suffer and die for our native country and for the kingdom of Jesus. Oh! walk softly, all ye people, walk softly; for God is among us, and the Searcher of Hearts is trying us as the gold is tried.

www.ingramcontent.com/pod-product-compliance
Lightning Source LLC
Chambersburg PA
CBHW030914260626
47169CB00008B/2847